Land's End

by

Jay Ruvolo

Land's End
Copyright © 2015 by Jay Ruvolo

This is a work of fiction.

Published by Piscataqua Press
An imprint of RiverRun Bookstore, Inc.
142 Fleet Street | Portsmouth, NH | 03801
www.riverrunbookstore.com
www.piscataquapress.com

Printed in the United States of America

ISBN: 978-1-939-7398-89

TABLE OF CONTENTS

A DREAM OF GRANDMOTHER

How many days, how many ways, how many
More how manies do I get to ask?
I watch you looking as if all depth
In a mirror were not an illusion. I
Reflect on reflections, what is in is on,
Another dream of Grandmother dead.
Hands bent, hands knotted, black and white photos
Of her I had taken, I recall how
Remembering was. I turn on the light
In our room; you say to turn it off, dreaming
The fear of what you might have seen — gray for days —
A skeleton face in review. I insist
On the light, how else am I going
To see? You dress in the mirror, I have
Been so already. "Don't pace," you warn, gazing
At the wall opposite me, I stare
At the common disarray. You do count
On me to be patient, a luxury
You indulge to excess. Downstairs outside
In front, we wait for the ride to Queens,
A cousin we see once a year. You make
Me buy flowers up the block, the man
With no English at the corner stand, flowers
In bunches, or to pick by ones. "No baby's
Breath." I say, "Turn the paper on the reverse,"
The tacky flower pattern hidden, "Leave
The inside-white outside." A breeze blows,
The flap folds, petals bend, our ride comes — I
Sit in the back to the cemetery.
I look up and out the rear window, leafless
Branches webbing the sky overcast

For miles, "Gray in grief for Grandmother,"
I say. You neither speak nor nod your head.
I cradle the roses in my arms as
We go, your face falling off petal
By petal, features peeling . . . the roses
Are black, black roses, black, not red. I expect
Black stems, black thorns to black petals. I hold
Them in my lap, tips of fingers keeping
An absent time. The roses, eleven,
Not twelve; yes, eleven flowers roses
O'clock, the funeral is this morning.

WITHOUT SIGNS

I wish I could say what it was that I
Remembered about you, watching you stand
With your back to the wind, the sun just above
The line of horizon, one hundred
Eighty degrees of ocean. A gull
Hovers, holding onto a crab, legs dangling
From its beak. A bit of salt spray, several
Grains of sand in my mouth, waves weaving
Symmetry as wings do in flight. The ocean
Here terrible, tumult over tumult.
Other gulls have come squawking, frighteningly
Ungainly birds. I whisper the mirror,
Suspicions in succession, I imagine
The Albatross. I find more wounds, the skin
I inspect, tips of fingers walking,
Expecting to uncover what you mean
To tell me. You are afraid of the gulls,
I fear shards for weeks after dropping a glass.
I know how words break, the glass broken,
I cultivate new scars, keeping open,
My eyes, the shadows I see oblong,
Fingering them as I do, they will not
Heal; the shadows I toss, newly found stones
At the sun. You said you remember the stones
We used to collect on the beach. I did
Not notice you had taken my hand.

SURF'S EDGE

I never used the slingshot I had when
I was a boy. I couldn't imagine
Shooting squirrels with rocks, *The stones, John; John,*
The stones. Vermont summer granite, I stumbled
Uphill, slipping on a snake after trout.
She is always the same different woman,
Another morning at the shore, summer
Vacation, Montauk, I walk surf's edge
Into town for coffee . . . croissants, almond
Beautiful — two for us every morning, we
Walk an extra few miles. I no longer
Wonder if I should have wondered if I
Should have remained the same man — a cousin
Whose name I have forgotten chopped the snake
With his fishing knife. How could I remain the same
Man that I was? I might have shot them wildly —
Trepidations here are serious,
The sands under my feet, another ocean
Wave coming over — pebbles are handier
Than the stones . . . and I try to skim them
On the ocean as I had when I was
A boy in the Berkshires on the lakes we
Would swim, Onota, I remember . . .
The stones, John, the stones. Alliterative,
Are they not; sticks and stones, you know? I broke
My bones when I was a boy, how many
Times my arm in a cast, jumping out
Of trees to slide down snowy hills. A flat
Stone in the shape of a surfboard on the beach
At Ditch Plains, I uncovered. I explore

Carefully once more my skin—sands matted,
The edge of low tide, neither wounds nor words
Recollected, a gull lands to hunt
For the clams its beak's engineered to open.

Dinosaurs, she says. *Prehistoric, are*
They not? She asks. I agree. She matches
My pace side-by-side walking, step-for-step steps—
My mouth opens her mouth, broken shells, broken
Words, a crab has fallen from the beak
Of a gull. Of course rhyme has its own reasons—
We are alone waiting for dawn. A glow
Increasing above the ink of the sea,
The line of horizon wobbles faintly,
The red-orange-yellow smolder broadens.
The gulls are hungry, more come squawking.
I keep thickly unforgettable, the scars
I have found, searching me as I have combed
The beach for stones—recollecting me
I realize has other implications.

A TRAVELER'S ADVISORY

Another vanishing point arises,
My view—what I say I do when I see—
To come to be or not to come to be.
Other questions I have posed, newly poised—
Another journey on a road I said
Might be the one. Knowing is beneficial,
Newly acquired affectations—I
Will weep for my father in the years
To come; for my mother too, I remember
Her laugh and how she lost her sense of humor
In the months before she died. I would have
Liked to have said something sensitive
About the details of her life, everything
Is in the details—Michelangelo's
"Dying Slave" leaps at me from across
The gallery. Life's lived in the minutes,
I tell you, the Louvre was more impressive
Than I had suspected it would be. I
Tell you how my life's been laid out, step by
Step at tide's edge, our way to Ditch Plains,
The Hoo Doos hauntingly above us looming.
We imagine we can walk to the lighthouse.
I recall lines drawn when I was a boy, stick
Figure sketches—*Nothing so difficult,*
Pablo said, *as a line.* I glimpse an old
Woman painting at the edge of a cliff
Above us. Footprints fade in the distance.

EURYDICE EXTENDING

White foam caps on the waters as far out
As my eye can see, we watch the surfers
Surf, ocean waves rising higher, we make
It to Ditch Plains for hot dogs, with relish,
From the truck. At the edge of the cliffs
Of Shadmoor, I guided you over the rocks
In the surf. Itsy-bitsy, we play,
The spider now in your palm. I took your
Hand; I reached behind me without looking
Back. I slowed down for you to catch up.
I saw them moving in time with the breeze
Blowing mutely from behind the window,
The branches of the tree between me
And the lamppost. Eyes fixed on the streetlight—
The bedroom window opens east. I too
Look out the window after a nightmare.
I imagine a stampede—elephants
In a herd through the part in the curtains,
Another lamppost blaring—Who are you
There in the middle of the night—? I doubt
Ever having believed what it is I
Think I imagined of you, falling behind
As you do—tortuously extending
Beyond comprehension, I turn to look,
And what I see hopefully—I lose.

INTO THE PARALLAX

Palms in Barcelona, palms in Miami,
Palms in the Keys, west in search of Papa,
I heard bulls gored three people yesterday.
We made it to *Plaza de Torres*
In Madrid. I found myself rooting
For the bulls. I look behind, another snaking
Line extended, seagull footprints in the sands,
An indecipherable algorithm—
I recall a tavern for lunch by the sea,
Grilled octopus with *Galician white.* We talk
About Columbus and the Maid of Orleans,
Jimenez and I. Columbus saw ships
Descending into the horizon,
Devotion I offer to my mother's
Namesake—I stand on a few thousand pieces
Of shattered shells, feet sinking in the sands,
Salt water loosens calluses. I know
The ships I see do fall off the edge
Of the world—what compelled Isabella
To send Columbus? The ground I walk on
Is flat; facts, facts and more facts. I find me
Wishing I could read your face; your gaze
Amazes me, Joan of Lorraine now comes
Into view, I close my eyes. I see you
Also standing alone facing the sea—
Your feet sucked in the quick of the surf soaked sands.

TATTERED COPIES

Your hands on your hips like one of Cezanne's bathers
On the cover of a copy of Whitman's
Leaves of Grass I used to carry with me
All tattered now on a shelf. I see you
In the clouds, I watch you in the sky, shifting
Lines abruptly in the wind, unable
To withstand another wave — I see you
In one overcoming me, another
That about tumbles me — how to withstand
The ocean waves one after another
Perpetually, standing in the surf,
Watching you, predawn, in the gloaming, your
Features, less what they are, what they were — contours
In the dark, silhouettes, definite, what
Could they be? I lift from the surf a cracked
Conch to my ear, I hear what I half expect
I will not, the hole in its side affecting
The acoustics. I told a boy I knew
The same would be true for his trumpet. I
Think I hear your voice in the waves, the draw
Of each wake back into the sea . . . I turn
To look for you in the rush of waters,
Now gurgling, my throat is hoarse, I gargle
With warm water and lemon — how many
Did you buy? I do not ask. Questions leading,
My throat, it still bothers me. Your voice, I
Hear your voice. I've been hoarse for weeks, I fear
Cancer, I whisper to you, asking you
If you had asked me anything in the waves,
If you — had you cast your voice to the sea?
And you say you did not speak to me, say

To me anything that could have been swallowed
By the waves. I say no more, watching you
Gaze at the clouds on the horizon, telling
Me you think that they look like white hippos.
I do not know if I believe you when
I do not ask you who I should have to be
To put to you important questions, always
Impertinent, new world inquiries
Following old world inquisitions.
Columbus set sail from Barcelona — I
Touched my hand to the foot of his statue
By the sea. No more bullfights — Barcelona,
The year before we arrived. We were staying
Five minutes away on foot. I recall
My disappointment. People without
Imaginations in Cataluña
Campaigning against bullfights. I recollect
The spectacle of Plaza de Torres
In Madrid, *Los Franquistas* alive and
Well — *how ugly* — behind us in the stands.

Madrid was beautiful, keeping an eye
Peeled for Penelope Cruz. I wish I
Could have sailed with Columbus, no guilt
For colonialism, standing as
I did thankfully at his statue facing
The sea. I open my mouth at the ebb
Of low tide, a ship bound for Oran
Disappears below the horizon.
Another wave swallows my voice. A storm
Hovering off the Carolinas —

Impossibly humid in New York,
The barometer drops. I am still proud
Of the Italian *Colombo* — tropical
Depression, sheets of moist air coming up
The coast; salt air does my throat good — a cure
For cancer, I must have found. I wrote
A poem about rooting for the bulls
And how the matadors were brave nonetheless.

DARWIN'S FINCHES

Length cannot tire as do her arms, ends
Do not justify what we imagine.
Too long, I endure my nature, reflecting
Other manners, other means, other mirrors
Held up, this one crumbles in a moment,
Shards fall to my feet. The birds, their nest, piece
By piece, bit by bit—I know her, who holds
It; she knows me too. Nothing but the thing
In itself, the thing in itself, vanity
Amid the darkness. A candle flame,
Flickering; in her lap—Alas! a skull,
I see. She gazes at the skull. I hear
The birds early morning on the fire
Escape. I recognize the skull, another
Moment, I watch her lap askance. My head,
My head, I long to lay my head down
Upon her lap. Her hair's long, it's full, it's
Thick . . . flowing tresses cover her face, her
Head bowed as if praying. Her arms fatigue,
Held up as they are, as they were, she sits
And bows her head again. Gorgeous, her arms,
Their arc, sexy sleeveless—I watch them shaking
Slightly. Jaggedly falling, shards fall—
Another mirror crumbles. I remember
Them at the opening, Darwin's finches,
It seems she wants to relieve herself.
I have been preoccupied at best. New
Questions beget yet other questions—all
Of it in the origins, you know—what
Birds are these? Outside the lone window facing
East, the fire escape platform, morning

Coffee; I move closer. They fly away,
Or below to their nest on the cable box.

ON THE ORIGIN OF A FILM

Everything is a web of life and death,
A sobering reassurance I get
From reading Darwin. I put him down
To order another coffee and donut.
Telling tales I had decided against,
Other shows I have seen—I will buy one
Of the Audubon books at Barnes and Noble,
Union Square. How could I so soon? I will
Not. I do not. I enjoy the stories
I tell, I do. I wish I knew my birds
Much better than I am going to . . . what
I see gathering around me, every-
Around-me-where, disarray—a future
Film I might never make, the curtains up
Then down, all of a sudden, I take
Videos of them, the shadows of branches
On the curtains made in India,
Silhouettes in time with the breeze outside.
The sound of the birds in flock on the fire
Escape. The morning sun peeks through the leaves—
With my camera, manual soft focus,
Always black and white film, other features
Of a new vague desire, tenebrous
In the stark checkerboard of light and dark.

ORIGAMI BREAKFAST

A flame atop a candle flickers,
The mirror echoes it as it burns. Her
Vanity with baubles, other verities
Scattered, how much is penitence worth? Beliefs
First held as a child. Questions fold, how
Do they fold? Like paper, like flowers,
Origami arts and crafts on Parent's Day.
I watch a kindergarten class perform—
Are they swans or are they cranes? Fold a thousand
And make a wish, a girl from Japan told
Me on Fifty-seventh Street. Birds outside
My window this morning, a gathering
Frenzy, I hear them on the fire escape,
The nest they built atop the cable box.
The sun peeks its head over the buildings
And the trees. Coffee sipped in mottled shade.

ALGERIAN FLOWERS

Magret de Canard at Jules, medium,
Never well. The waitress from Lyon lights
The votive. The *Puligny Montrachet*
Needs to come up, white burgundies, too cold
And they close, roses and cunts. The bucket
Of ice water I leave for a cut stem —
Roses, red roses, he cradles as he
Sells them, a photo of him I have at home
In an album I bought on sale. I recall
Small-talking in French 1 on the weekends
Before Nine-eleven, my Amazigh
Friend and I. I buy one, just one, red,
Never yellow, only one red rose
Every time. Our table, in the corner,
Sitting by each other, she and I, beneath
A movie poster of Jean Gabin —
La Bête Humaine. We listen to Jazz,
A band from Marrakech, the roses now
In the bucket on the table I see
In the mirror on the wall on our right.

INTERCESSION

I shampoo my hair, I rinse my body
Longer, a whirlpool of re-memory,
Bubbles bursting, the vortex in the tub
Turns. Time dilates, the abyss opens wider.
I watch the water run down the drain. Wine,
Over the years, has passed quickly, a decade
Or more ago, how far has it been since
My last—what I whisper in the dark. Her
Forefinger and thumb, how she reaches for crust,
Breaks a bit from a piece. Low-light shots have
Been my forte—an extra votive set
By the basket, an opposable thumb
On the heel to be buttered. Confessions
Are not for the weak; impossibly said,
It has been too long—words I cannot say.
Nobody holds what I can by candle
Light—one-fifteenth of a second, aperture
Set to f/1.4. The camera lens,
Manual focus. Her fingers, a silent
Motion picture still—elegant, long, tapered—
Candle flame reflected off her nail polish
In monochrome. This night across from each
Other at our table by the banquet.
We sit side by side in the corner—
The votive lights lit by our waitress.
Her wrist silent, still, delicate, bones
I imagine more fragile than they are.

THE GREENHOUSE EFFECT

Failures I do not manage are minor
Compared with those my neighbor messes up.
A thousand motes in my own, yet those people,
I know them and theirs, these people; I do
Not need to ask who they are, with the beams
In their eyes — I see what I do; a man
Without sin should cast the first stone. Around
And around in my head, listening,
As I do, as I have done, to someone
Other in my head, *Should, Would and Could are*
Three fools wandering the world — no one
In a glass house should throw the stones I have
Collected at the beach, the cliché demands
Another must do, another would or
Would have to do or not to do, what I
Do not need others to tell me. I throw
Stones, have gotten good at throwing bricks,
Heavy old-way baked bricks I throw like
Looney Tunes let loose on those who cannot
Imagine I imagine what they are.

ENGENDERING

Angels have no gender, no sex, no one
Has ever seen a naked angel. One
Should never without caution; I assume
It does not matter when. I could not tell
What or where. I cannot now recall who.
No lover ever knows another let
Alone the other. An echo resounds —
Empty apartments, empty heads. Who asks
The questions I should have asked? I never
Know exactly how. I cannot tell — I hear
Wind chimes next door. The circumambient
Dark tightening, her voice voices fear, my
Fear, whose voice I do not recognize — I
Know that Truth is tautological.
Vanity is charity, I do hear
Another voice say that one should never
Without caution; how do we make up our
Petty truths? Up is up and down is down
As good is good is not bad. Everyone
Else's future is always brighter, more
Clichés for me to live by — good is up
And up is surely brighter than down should
Be. In the dark, I see only light that breaks.

A MAN LONELY GAZING AT CLOUDS

The birds eat Hansel and Gretel's brainstorm,
I remember the ball of string unravels
For Theseus — I let go — everyone I
Become — I become without gain, an arrow
Flies as it flies. Greater than one I am,
Singularly plural, no interest
Bearing in being anymore — not to be
The gain again, more adding and subtracting,
Dividing as I do . . . the summit's reached
By reaching. This new addition amazes
Me; with you without you with me — how I
Figure to find myself, neither in this
To be or not, I take my life as neither
Slings nor arrows — I become other than
Myself in my becoming — only
To be myself, this lethargy of questions
Posed, lines with hooks into the sea, every
String is strung, engrossing. A slothful gain,
Wanting is everything I had learned. I
Manage to achieve what I want what I
Need to want — my identity apart from
A-part-of. A mirror face at every
Turn appears. The string I have brought inside
The labyrinth stretched. Morning after morning,
Dawn shadows cast, a part of apart
From reflections . . . all about refractions
Contained — Identity spells ID Entity.

WHAT REMAINS

Clouds have come thickly, I do what I can
To see you. All I have done with or without
You, other themes, variability,
The boy I was listening to Mozart
I am repeating, variations
On yet other themes—once waiting for the sun—
Waves come quickly in succession it seems,
How long have they been coming like this?
Clumps of seaweed mark the edge of high tide,
Another tumult threatens to topple
Me. I walk the minor cut cliffs in the beach—
Standing as I have come to do, feet sucked
Into surf-sands, the ebb of low before
Me—dinosaurs peck for clams. I pause
With coffee and croissant in hand. The last
Wake extends about twenty feet from my feet.
I have stumbled in the surf before—
For what else remains of me, for what
I have left going inside, for every
I-to-I I have—my eyes have…I see
Me diving headlong into a wave.

ENTRY BY ENTRY AFTER ENTRY

The *I* fills out line by line by entry
After entry — I whisper the prayers
I have forgotten I did not remember. I
Think I might remember yellow. Colors
Come as symbols come. Lights flashing red, blue
And green — I bought a set of yellow coffee
Mugs from Fish Eddy on Hudson years ago.
Incessantly beeping, I hear beeping —
Hooked up to machines, machines beeping
Incessantly. She cannot sustain herself,
And so without the work of these machines . . .
I imagine I hear her voice. I keep
Her going for me, not for anyone
Else. Hope against hope is useless hoping,
The hospital staff works hard to drive home
The idea that I should let her die.
The culture of death is upon us —
ISIS should be no surprise. Three weeks I
Am there every night next to her — I
Do not stay until dawn as I did
With my dad, having stayed with my dad
In a hospital that hated the idea
They had to serve him. *Protestant and Jew*
Have the same problem, so I've been told, image
After image — I am there word by word
After word, *Full of grace . . .* what graces my
Life? I see their common problem daily.
I have never wished it could be otherwise.

SURGERY

Smoke from incense rises, I watch the priest
At the altar, a *Christ Pantocrator*
Fresco on the ceiling in the apse. I
Listen close for the Latin I know,

Agnus Dei qui tollis . . . kneeling
In the pews, I try to pray as I once
Knew how to pray. The apparatus
As much as her face, my gaze in mind wide-eyed,

The world and her have become one. Every
Singularly minute-by-minute thing,
Sorting a life *be now my rock*—Sisyphus
Becomes me. Measuring by mimicking

Attempts to help? All things in disarray
Here at her home, more decisions to make,
Made again, her landlady steals her
Deposit. I have not summed all; I need

More plastic-bags. I throw so many things
Away, all accounts left assumed, assumptions
Are easy; *ergo ego*, I presume.
I overcome myself, again, souvenirs

I collect. Odd baubles assembled
On a shelf. I know why surgeons cannot
Perform their surgery on family.
Everything I touch tonight, the scalpel's blade.

AN AGE OF DISCOVERY

I am tired of asking the questions
I pretend I believe I am supposed
To be asking. No one knows how, really;
No one ever does. Nearly two weeks
To prepare, no higher functions. What I
Fear next, my mother's voice, I weep for her
Death, the infant me, she leaves my crib. My
Pen runs dry on the page. Words and more words,
I try to assemble myself, what I
Need to be. I recollect having failed,
No calendars or clocks to mark the passing,
The journal entries I write I leave
Undated. I recall the telescope
Lenses I kept in a box wrapped in a bag—
What has happened by hour or by date? I
Wrote nothing for three weeks as my dad lay
Dying. Answers newly at random, I
Cannot tell what I recall having thought—
It is thinking that makes us human. It's
A choice, *To human or not to human.*
I recall my mother staying awake
All night by a schnauzer as he lay dying
On the floor of the bathroom at the foot
Of the radiator until dawn when
He did die—yet other answers come
At the ready—would anything else be
Any the less? In a flash, I flip
A coin, heads or tails, tails or heads—the world,
Mister Lanier, I too know is lit by
Lightning. Nowadays, I fear glass, one shatters
Darkly, I walk into childhood, I

See the moon through the telescope that mom
And he bought for me . . . my dad then pointing
To The Sea of Tranquility, *There, that*
Shadowy patch I learned was *to the lower*
Right of the Man on the Moon's face, patches
Of shadows cast by the ridges of
The craters we once had thought were watery
Seas — *That's where we're going to land.*

SACRED AND PROFANE

Chalk outlines mark the asphalt by my home.
Infinite possibility, you know,
Is an avalanche waiting to bury
Us. The games we played in youth we play again,
Sacred and profane, a newer hop-scotch,
Eternal return, you understand,
I understood — the impossibility
Of motion is real, *the arrow flies*
As it flies — it proves moving from here to there's
Impossible. Everything recedes
Via the midpoint; from A to B
By way of the midpoint and to another
Midpoint by way of yet another midpoint.
I tunnel my way through many miles
Of me — I tell myself to count the hours,
Time and space are occasional. One two
Three, I watch them pass. All that passes
In passing — the world is always *gira*
Gira. The merry-go-round goes 'round and
'Round — Franco used to say, *Gira gira,*
The world I was supposed to know. We spend
Some time together apart, who are we
Now? A silent question remains. Every
Line of differing lengths, each infinite
Of points — each line the same size as others,
I tunnel my way through miles of me,
I imagine I arrive at you.

THE BODHISATTVA OF GRAVITY

She sits beneath The Tree of Knowledge
Preaching the gospel of throwing dice.
I look into her eyes snake eyes
In the garden that houses the tree.
I too sit beneath the tree as it grows
Growing faster than trees grow.
Looking through me, I stand in the window
A world behind the pane,
Separate traces of days removed,
Dreams residual more remote.
She holds a mirror up to the world,
I cannot tell if I sleep or wake.
New skins I shed old snake in my grass.
The garden flowers bloom aloud I manage to resist.
She wonders about the I-am that I become
A truth to tempt me.
Someone to tell me, I sense
That vanity finds this tree.
New verities I know as well, the blossoms fall.
Petal by petal again to meet new gains,
The apple tree with real fruit ripening.
Evening has come, I taste the apples.

FRAGILE LETTERS

For Hart Crane

I imagine I want the letters I
Have written to friends returned so I can
Revise them, mumbling to myself something
About Dylan, *How do you do, Mister*
Thomas, another pint at the White Horse,
Oh! Yes, Bill, the apples, Bill, the apples.
Building a play in Bill Packard's workshop,
HB Studio on Bank Street. I tried
To tread gently, echoes of apples
One-by-one falling, into the past,
Into the half-full-with-water cedar
Barrel out back . . . I must look more carefully
To see what I should see, there are many
Have-to(s) for you, for me—I remember
Hart—the apples we picked one chilly fall
In the orchard. I watch her hands handle
The apples from the trees in the garden,
I see the crab apple tree in Aunt Anna
Mae's front yard, branches, thick and full with leaves
Dark green and ready fruit, *The benefits*
Of a rainy spring, Mister Van Dam said,
One summer, decades ago, in the Berkshires.

A VALENTINE

"His soul shall taste the sadness of her might [...]"
"Ode on Melancholy,"
John Keats

I look in
Your eyes

I imagine
Me in your
Eyes

I see me
In your eyes

I know me
In your eyes,

Your eyes, the world
Enough

Full of sorrow

Your eyes.

I love you

You see.

TAUTOLOGY

Absence is absence, in the way a pig
Is a pig and not a table, unless
Dead and stuffed and put in front of a sofa.
What picture books do you put on a pig?
I wonder now the table a table
And not a pig, coffee-table books
For coffee-table pigs. A woman is
A woman and not her stuffing. My mother's
Arms bloated, swollen fingers black and blue,
The nurse comes to stick her again. I cannot
Keep my eyes off her swollen wrist, her name
Tag ready to burst. I cannot help her.
I write on the page, the journal comes
To its end, every conclusion ready
To overflow. I wonder what I would
Do if there were taxidermy for women,
Keep her at home standing or sitting I
Would have to decide in a corner perhaps
Which room for sure I would consider
The vantage on entering, decisions,
Decisions, the dam bursts. A woman is
A woman and not her stuffing. Dead pigs
Used as tables before dead sitting people
On sofas, dead sitting women as chairs —
Function supplants form — women are women.

FARCE

She's dead, I said, under my breath, *Tu n'es*
Pas un poulet farci, Maman. A woman
Is a woman and not a dead bird, I
Used to make extra in a baking pan
For my mother. I always stuff the bird
On Thanksgiving, corn bread, sausages, apples
And sage. I don't keep the machines going
In the name of Hope. I play at effort,
This farce for sure, yes, stuff the bird— in French
Cooking, *la farce* is the stuffing, I saw
The CAT scan. How can I hold out hope? I
Do not ask. Her brain's been stuffed by blood—I
Keep her beyond the protests of nurses.
Love is doing what you know you can't do.

BROKEN OFF OR APART

The wine we drank at *Il Colosseo*,
Lacryma Christi, Vesuvius grapes,
Chilled white with *calamari fritti*,
A *tre colori* salad with olive
Oil and lemon — soft shell crabs *francese*,
Spectacular. Opposable thumb
To opposing index, pulling off and out
Of the bag a piece of croissant, remnants
Of paper-cup coffee to my lips. I
Walked back from watching the surf with toes's edge
To the wakes to sit down on the huge log
That had washed up on shore from a storm I
Have since forgotten when — what year, nonetheless —
We were glad to have found it, this log
To sit and eat on. I recollect me
Once having been a tree missing a limb,
This log once a branch of a tree, humongous —
A play I had written before — *what if*
I were a tree? How many years I could
No longer say — I try to see me clearly —
I never see me in my dreams, eyes peering
At the world as if through a mask. I think
I remember the tears of Jesus, fixed
Position always, on the life-like plaster
Face of Christ — or was it marble? I do
No longer recall sitting in the pews —
I close my eyes; I imagine I see
Me gazing at the altar, the crucifix
Hanging where I received First Holy
Communion, and later Confirmation.

HIGH DUNE GRASS

Summer evening has come; I stand in the gloaming,
Odd man is out, even Steven says, *You have*
To see that remaining the same is different.
The sun has dropped below the high dune grass, he adds.
Recollecting me, in a moment, diffuse rays
Of the setting sun through the gaps in the blades,
Pedestals toppled to get a better view, night
Was like day, day like night, rising from the east. Night
Rises, does not descend. I recall a parade,
Last Macy's Day, standing at curb's edge. Lear-like
Against the fury of the waves, I stand. One after
Another newer tumult to impress. I look
Once more to see what others see, seeing so much
More having seen, more than once when I was a boy,
The X-ray, part of the healing, I knew — my empty
Cup in the bag with crumbs. The circumference
Of my right radius — I thought I heard a branch
Snap. I'm not entire without the sea as the sea
Is as the sea does, I then do as I am — I
Do not wish I knew more than I know, or more than
I could know — all about what I do not understand,
Could never, about the sea — anything about
Me about the sea with the sea I could not know.

STRANGER STILL

To philosophize, I learned, was to learn
How to die. Why would anyone want to—I
Promise to come early—a pigeon I
Saw sat for hours outside her window—
The day after tomorrow—I did
Not see him land. An oblong shadow traced
The inside of her sill—a leap of faith,
I suspected. I asked, What was it?
Nonetheless, I have never been anything
Except fickle. What I learn to take,
Stealthily, in the middle of the night,
Her neurologist came to confirm brain-dead.
Passing hours, hours ticking—how long
Did the pigeon stay? Pigeons are doves, doves,
Pigeons—the Holy Ghost appears as a dove.
Picasso's dove, Noah's dove—the stones I
Acquire at the edge of the sea. I
Kiss an icon of Jesus and Mary
I have on the wall at home—the pigeon landed
Three days before I now think I know—
What do I know except one overriding
Fact—my mother did die in sorrow-birth,
Nine months to the day my father died.

RE-QUESTER

I barely recall my mother holding
My hand when I was a boy. I hold hers
Now until her heart stops beating. The doctor
Who comes to disconnect the tubes leaves
The room, she says I am a good son.
Embraces embracing, my arms wrapped around
Her, a boy not knowing his mother is
Not the whole of the world in laughter
And tears. I push my boy-head firmly
To her belly, her cheek presses close
To the soft spot of my skull. I hear words,
Crystal words falling in shards in her voice,
I love you too honey, she said. I think,
Therefore I imagine, I always went
Fishing with an *I-love-you-mommy* for bait.
I tried to mean something significant
In my journal, the pen I carry
With me wherever I go—I am—how
Am I? New questions to avoid answers.
The pen plays in staccato across
The page, invisible umbilicus
Divisible—hyperbole hampers
My way. I see things clearly out her window
Now the sun peeks from behind the clouds setting
Over Richmond, words fail as they have failed
Before, will fall or fail again—my speech
Continues, keeps its petty pace. Leaves this
October, especially colorful.
I wonder for a time about who she
Was, this She she becomes. God is He and
God is It—how can God be He, She and

It? You ask. Another theological
Inquiry performed by offering prayers—
A new Trinity arises there
For me to prefer—I do stand under
The weight of the world. He, She, and It
Together, all three in one . . . everything
Then absolved dissolves me. Heretics,
Though, they cannot receive absolution.

LOOKING HOMEWARD

Thorns a part of its beauty, the rose; I
Wring my hands around, other looks peeling
Layers, tearing-the-flesh ritual, eyes
Peer into other eyes, *Get it,* she said –
She saw its tail under the stove disappear.
Her eyes into mine as I explain how
The mouse will suffocate slowly, the eyes have it,
What to have? The mouse on the glue trap tied
Up. When's a rose, a rose, and not my love?

AT THE GRAVE

Imagination is eternity,
Eternity *not forever, forever*
Inside eternity. I do not
Imagine it possible, but cannot
Say it is impossible, drops dripping
Faintly, the blood dripping from thorn-pricks
In my palms. The theory of gravity
Rests on the displacement of space. I toss
Roses into her grave. I see me reading
Blake imagining me stealing, as I
Do, lines given lines taken lines reused
As Great Aunt Anna did ribbons and
Bows and the wrapping paper wrapped around
The gifts she would receive, I recall my dad's
Recitation of "Lycidas," a boy
By his side, an old tattered copy, more
Profoundly reading Milton, holding fast
To the Blake wonder I might not have had
If not for *Blake in Blake light with Blake madness . . .*
Reading Blake aloud in shopping malls—
Milton and Blake both addend the Bible,
I remember me saying to a group
Who had no idea what I was saying.

RELATIVITY PHYSICS

An angel's face in a cloud I see out
The window. I'm supposed to see angels
In the sky? The clouds, the white clouds, flattering
My sense of purity. The winding road
Turns the bus. The angles on this angel
Are shifting each turn of the steering wheel,
A turn at representation. The face
Is now gone; obliquely, occluded
By the trees that pass the same speed as the bus.

FOLDS UNTANGLE

I have removed the veil, the folds have untangled,
I manage an I-to-I with me. I ask too much
Of too many too often. Another question
Raised raises other questions, my inquiries follow
An independent logic. How much of how many
Others too much could I request? Asking seems so
Much other than hoping, other than what wish I
Should keep. If I were asleep a hundred years,
I would not wake sooner, sleeping is one learned habit
I no longer indulge. Self-indulgence's indulgent.
By tautology again, the truth is revealed.
Of living with myself, I have not solved the problem.
It finds its solution—everyone in solution,
Dissolving, a sea of humanity absolves me.

NOT ONLY FOR HORSES

Nothing's for certain, everything's in doubt,
Always-polite, the new *politique*;
I hear nothing but nihilism pure,
Out of human mouths mouthing human words,
American Mammon, Moloch's America,
America, America! Monstrosity America,
Terminally totalitarian
Capitalist—everybody's Money's
Nigger in America. What else can you
Do with a slave that dreams of the freedom
Of dreaming? *Why should slaves have dreams?* "Cut off
His fucking balls," of course. "Chop off his fucking
Toes," you must. Brutalize the slave that dreams,
Every slave has to know. Forever is
A condition of slavery. Masters
Cannot punish slaves with added years
Of servitude. What slave would not trade his
Slavery for serfdom, a peaceful, far
Less violent serfdom—*why can't niggers
Now be happy being welfare serfs,
They are no longer chattel slaves, are they?*
America, America, everywhere her
Serfs, everywhere new serfs in our kinder,
Gentler America—America, now Moloch's
America, serving Mammon as God.
Feudalism's freedom for the chattel slave.

BROTHERS OF A KIND

John Doe lives again, takes off the toe tag,
Misspeaks his name, calls himself by another.
A trail of crumbs I leave behind, I do
Imagine myself Hansel imagining
Himself Percival. A ball of string would
Have been better. How is the forest not
A maze? Amazing sights in the woods. Long
In the afternoon, the shadows of the hills.
The Minotaur's present in the shade
Of the forest paths I take, I took, I
Did know how to get back to Aunt Anna
Mae's. Coming back, everything put back.
The compass in my head, we never get
Lost in foreign cities. All else around
Me around us a part of us. Every
Slave lives in a labyrinth. Every
Revolution returns to its beginning,
Around and around, how many before
Theseus came. The Minotaur first lurking
Then hiding, avoiding each turn I take,
Stepping carefully gently, as I think
I cannot know a thing the slave or
The Minotaur knows. Who is like unto this slave?
The Minotaur asks me by surprise. I
Imagine he thinks he knows something I
Haven't considered. I'd introduce him
To Caliban if ever I had the chance.

MADNESS AT BABEL

Every baby born has the ability
To speak any language—learning one
As we grow is to forget every other,
What I intended to say in the first
Place, by saying so much less than what else
I have said, having failed to realize only
The failure of words when I try to mean
What I say at—how I learned my lessons
Well, attention to the details, garnered
By having been told not choosing is
A choice, the dream of being exists
With newer clichés about tautologies—
They would still be trite. A link of chain is
A link of chain is a link to how many
Crows have gathered outside our window?
I can imagine slavery is
Slavery is slavery, always the same
Around forever evermore. If it
Were not for this special reflex I have,
That would otherwise have been spoken,
A speech that makes me choke on the words, when
Every rite I speak holds back what I keep,
Other clichés would abide what I avoid.
I have other ideas about Truth.
Nothing new under the sky, the clouds, old
Winds that blow, recurring signs, familiar motifs
From how old the earth has been. I do not
Imagine that there should be another
Method I could go mad developing.

DAWN BY HITHER HILLS

I read the changing colors, how long
Before dawn, I remember a sun that
Peeked above the sea one summer, dawn
Is further north in the fall, comes up over
The land of the South Fork. I have read your
Eyes, other mornings, black pools this day you are
Backlit by the sun now rising, an orange
Disk your head cannot eclipse. A photograph
Taken by me on our spot on the beach,
Hail to thee, Oh Ra! The giant log all
Of a sudden one summer, having come
After a storm. Dawn is what it does, does
What it says — we rose fifteen minutes
Before the sun, passing beneath a trellis
Of red roses out back in the dark.
Later, we thought we would walk on the road
Along the back of the dunes, almond
Beautiful, silhouette, we finish,
Morning sun, our croissants. Standing, muted
By the wind, naked camera opened
Eyes — red is black in the dark. I close them
And just as quickly once more I open
Them, your face, shrouded, I pick at the almond
Slivers in the bag, changing colors read.

INTER-TEXT

Your body's shadow five times as tall as you.
Less enthusiastic about what will
Be—are you able to reach as high? No
Sense in sensing any more. Am I taller
In the mirror? Am I *I am* with you?
I stand on the shoulder of a dwarf
To get a better view. Am I as tall,
Alone? No one in the dark . . . Orpheus
Descends into Hades—*Don't look back,* I
Tell you as we cross the rocks where the beach
Narrows at the foot of the cliffs. How low
Would I go? How long to walk—Eurydice
Fades—to the lighthouse we are bound, have I
Lost you as well? As you do, as you are,
As you will be, more especially well
Mannered. You are as tall as you once were,
As I once could have hoped. Your body's
Become five times as tall as you in shadow.
More than in thought, to think or not to think
Must be the question. How we think about
What we feel—Hamlet is Cartesian,
You know. I am, therefore I think. What I
Feel more importantly—imperatively
More—thus what I think, now when I do, that I
Do—the moment I find myself no longer
Wishing, no longer hoping, futilities
Only fitting. Another fantasy
Of me. I find myself filling the hours,
Alone with or without you, fractured images
Coming back obliquely. Minutes, really. *Don't
Look back,* you warned. I could not help myself.

THE MIRROR

for George de La Tour

A boy who first sees her in a room full
Of Rubens — I have been to this room
At the Met, at the Louvre, I recall
Visits to other museums in other
Cities. I watch her sitting, her vanity,
Alone in her penitence — how could it
Be otherwise, fixed on the flame, reflected
In the mirror. I am, she is — the boy
Is wide-eyed in a room full of Rubens.
No one has yet done for flesh what he had.
A candle burning brightly, Magdalene
Alone in circumambient darkness,
The candle doubled in the mirror,
A *doppelganger* flame flickeringly
Frozen. Alas! In her lap, we see the skull.
I sit on the bench alone in the middle
Of the gallery, her gaze fixed on the hollows.
Whose skull? I ask. I know I have come
To the grave before — every time I visit
The Met. He knows her I think he knows I
Do. The boy knows her name, my name — I know
This boy's name. What's in a name — how many
Arrows by others would not have pierced
Sebastian's hide — a statue I recall
In old Madrid we passed on our way
To *La Sanabresa* for lunch. A saint
By any other name could never smell
As stone? *Words are what we make them say.*

WHITE BURGUNDY WITH DUCK
IS ONLY OUTDONE
BY WHITE BURGUNDY
WITH LOBSTER DRIZZLED WITH BUTTER

May I lay my head upon your lap? I
Spy her crotch, she sits in shorts, Ophelia
Feared Hamlet was saying something unsaid,
Who would question what I know about it?
Culpability by the Cherry Blossoms —
I watch her walking in the garden,
Muted steps, I look to a photo of her.
Other names come to me in a dream; I
Spell them out on paper next to stick figure
Doodles. She walks away, silently —
I see her legs before I do her head.
We decide, we do, to have *Meursault*
With the duck breasts medium, never well.
I am, she is, I smell think a sweet rose.

ANOTHER PORTRAIT

The last of the white burgundy, I finger
The stem of my glass, I forget how
To imagine what I need to see
To be able to lie to myself.
An afternoon a decade ago — only
Wine ever as beautiful as cunt. I
Cannot count the shadows of the visions
That parade — another portrait remembered,
Circumambient darkness with the skull
She holds in her lap, the skull, *Ma belle belle*
Douce Madeleine — the stone walls are a bit
Slimy. She gazes at the seeping walls —
As drops of a rose wine from *Languedoc*
We liked stain the lapel of my white shirt

GRAVEYARD GOD

I am sure he does not remember his name—
What's in his name? I asked. I paused. I thought
To ask again, the question sticks in my teeth.
His name by any other—would he not be
Himself if he were called by another?
I am who I am even under
The forgetful watch of amnesia, no?
I once imagined not remembering who
I am, I was—when was I ever
As I am? I am never who I am
In constant flux I sometimes believe being
Is in perpetuity. I have learned
To ask other questions, sniffing hounds,
At the hunt. Questions *are* like hounds, like shitting
Dogs—a load of fresh dog shit he calls a rose.
He finds himself mesmerized by her shape.

DOG SHIT BY THE NAME ROSE

By any other name she would be
Equally fuckable, he says. The shadows
Quaver. He pauses to watch her shadows
On the wall in time with the candle flame
In time with the breeze through the window.
He turns to her and recalls a portrait
By Vermeer he had in a book in his
Room, a good set of prints, the form of her
Dress as it hangs on her . . . everything
About her long flowing hair past her
Shoulders. He turns to the shadows, not yet,
Imagination, nor yet again. What
Could have been made make-believe . . . by candle
Light all around the figures flickering,
He sees her eyes fixed. I see his eyes fixed.

LONELY AS A BOY IN A GRAVEYARD

I too fix my eyes, set them straight ahead
Onto her onto him, the function
Of vision becomes clearer . . . newly mastered
Observations function in place of other
Sights. All around me now, cemetery stones,
Long ago, I used to walk old graveyards—
It might seem to some, uncannily
The same as any other scene, graveyards—
I knew him, to be sure, this man by any
Other name, who imagined I saw and
Heard, as I had on a stage, there by a grave
In a cemetery, long ago, waiting
To bury my grandfather, another
Morning I recall warm, hazy, humid
June, in the Berkshires, at the open pit
For Aunt Anna Mae—I would read the names
And the dates and epithets carved in stone.

SITTING AT JULES
ON THE BANQUET
BY THE BAR
NEXT TO THE DOOR
LOOKING OUT ONTO SAINT MARK'S PLACE
THROUGH MY MANUAL FOCUS CAMERA
DURING A THUNDERSTORM
ACROSS FROM HER
WITH A BOTTLE OF *GIGONDAS* BETWEEN US
ONE SUMMER EVENING
MORE THAN A DECADE AGO

Hanging above the front door, over the sign,
JULES, a virtual stream off the lamp, hand
Held, one-fifteenth, how impossibly slow . . .
A photo of an evening thunderstorm,
The asphalt of Saint Mark's awash — hydroplane
Rising, torrential — a parked Mercedes
Wheel cropped just right — from the banquet by the bar
With the glasses from our *Gigondas*.

SERENDIPITY

For Anna Mae Grady Miller

The past is not past is not then but
Now here the way I think . . . Cousin Michael
In a bag from a mine outside of Danang.
His casket was closed. The same humid June,
I think ten days after, several now
Decades ago. *I don't know if I wish*
I could remember more than I do.
Shattered Berkshire images, I'm unable
To mend. I recollect collecting. What
Was it I had seen? Long ago drops
Of blood from my hands? *I heard her voice one night*
In the dark after she died. Her son will
Die thirty-five years after — I will not
Know until seven more years later,
By accident on the internet, Cousin
Buddy dead. *She called my name as she had*
When it was time to come to dinner. I
Recall the day she fell babbling in the kitchen,
How I ran straightaway out of her house
Into the middle of Yorkshire Drive.
I remember the hill that was Yorkshire
And the dirt road in a T at the top.
Dad came slowly after, right hand outstretched —
The hand I kissed the morning I said goodbye.

RECKONING

Blood seeks its level, I thought I remembered.
Droplets, little droplets, blood he seeks — blood.
We must atone for . . . blood, we imagine
We offer in sacrifice for the blood
We have let. Sewing is tedious. I
Am thankful the fabric is black. Tiny
Drops of blood falling, I tossed roses
Into the grave. Yawning — I have gotten
No sleep, I was up at three A.M. —
The Devil's hour mocks the death of Jesus.
A million waves, a million wings.
The pivot stays; an alignment, fixed
Remains previous. Everything turns
On its axis — future and past compete.

CAMERA OBSCURA

I gazed at a woman, at her portrait
On the wall—Vermeer was all about soft
Focus. I looked to see the boy who knew
Her, I have a series of solar grams
I keep in plastic sheaths in a binder
In a box at the bottom of a closet.
The principles of photography—
Vermeer the first artist influenced
By photography, his *camera*
Obscura — to see as he had seen,
Without the chemistry. My life has been
Unable to sustain itself, the edges
Of everything have become blurred, bound'ries
Opening, no longer understanding
Capillary walls. Time slows itself
To a standstill, I am sure I am, that
I could keep in mind better than you.
How much would I give? Everything like
The wind, openly winding, clocks ticking
Time, *of the clock* was sixty minutes long
Five hundred years ago, with one hand,
I woke in a dream holding an eraser.

WINTER FINGERS

Waiting, opened palm, opened eyes, recently
Awake, stunning hands, the photos I will
Recall, no one's hands like your hands, her hands,
A scene for sunrise. I watch the morning
Stage — sets I designed for one acts I had
Written (wrought) — the goddess, you know, you are
A goddess — I visit the Sanctuary
At Eleusis in a dream looking
For Persephone, but Demeter is
There guarding almost as fiercely as would
Medusa her lair, they do not, my hand,
A hand, I open and close my hand.
Fingers reaching, fingers stretching, touching
Thumb as they do, opposable and all,
It's no wonder we make reed instruments.

Words cannot, do not, will not . . . another
Itsy-bitsy spider, we play your fingers
In my palm, your palm, the fingers, I see
Their silhouettes, how delicately they
Appeared. I recall how gentle you were
With your hands, palm stroked, she said, you said, I
Lay the same down to sleep. Aristocratic,
She mentioned. Hands, elegant, fingers, long —
There should be more to say about hands,
About her hands, her fingers, the sun's now
Low in its arc across the sky.

I look
Out my window, mid-February morning,
Nimble fingers, shadow fingers; over

The buildings, the sun makes its way, the sky,
Across; the shadows of the branches this
Midwinter appear fingers on the wall.

PRIMITIVE RATTLE

She had forgotten how to laugh by the time
She was ready to die. It seems heroic
After the fall, how much my mother tried. I
Think of the bough that breaks, I watch the branches
Bend. I used to sing more when I was
A boy. All the chants from childhood come
Back, go away, rain that does not—rain, rain,
And all that coming and going again.
In the leaves in the trees outside, primitive
Rattle bringing rain, softly lifting
The curtains, my soul to take, in time
With the breeze that blows. On the wall shaking,
Silhouettes, skeleton fingers, winter
Bare branches, I see shadows, objects
In hand. All manipulation is by hand.
Her hand was cold as I held, unlike ice.

AND SO, GOODBYE

I see a knife cutting my mother's hand,
Frozen lobster tails under running water
In the sink of our East Flatbush ground
Floor apartment when I was five.

                                     I avoid
Talking about how big the tumor is
In my mother's uterus, how big it
Is purported to be, the blood in my
Mother's brain, I can talk about—

                                    My mother's
Hands like claws, like lobster claws, knotted hands,
Misshaped, arthritic—spasms I saw when
They locked on her, my mother's hands, her hands—
I think I can see my mother's hands, feel
My mother's hands taking my temperature
Off my forehead and face then ears—and so?

BLACKBIRDS

I knew I could not step into the same
River twice, the way up is the way down.
A girl said I was looking correctly
Obliquely when I saw a flock of black
Birds. I cannot step into the same ocean
Twice, I remembered having thought. I am
A crow squawking in the tree beyond
The tree, I imagined. It's impossible
For a crow to cross a field — birds and arrows,
Zeno's racetrack, you know, she said; you should
Read his paradoxes, she said. I used
Vincent's lines in drawing my birds in a sky
I drew in class. My third grade teacher
Witch said I could not draw. Crows, crows, more crows,
I bought a print of Van Gogh's last painting
For my first apartment. Out the corner
Of my eye. The shifting light of dawn,
Morning sun trying through the clouds to peek.
I saw it lift off from the topmost branch,
A raven — yes, a raven. It was too
Big, I imagine, to have been a crow.
It must have been a raven — what does
A raven look like? I did not ask her.
For sure it was a raven, she said, I
Remember. It was abrupt and loud when
It cawed. What I thought, could not matter.

MAGICAL REALITY

For Antonin Artaud

There are always ways we think we never
Think we could have thought, having thought without
Thinking what others think. I read from his
Letters to his brother Theo, a poster
Of his bedroom above my bed in my
Room in Brooklyn—Vincent was my name
For Confirmation. I knew she could never
Know she had no way to understand what
I seemed to understand without effort,
As I continued to imagine it
Possible for me to get from point A
To point B—standing under other thoughts—
The metro gets me to where I am going,
From one point A to another point B.
Be careful who your spiritual kin
Are, she said. I had no way to imagine
The world as she had. I had no way
To imagine not thinking Vincent was
My kin. I had no way not to have a way
To remain the way I would be *was*.

DROWN THE WAKING ANGUISH IN MOCK ALEXANDRINES

These poems are for no one, for no one can know them.
I am no one now, as you are no one here,
As I am no one everywhere—nobody, anybody
Is everyone—no one is who he is, when or
Where he is only one—no one will read them,
These poems that are for no one. No one will read them,
These poems that cannot be read because these poems are
Not for you, for me, for anyone myself—
Nor for anyone else—matter or matter not—
Any he, any she, any it—one by one
After one—it cannot know them, will never
Know them. Who is like unto the poet—these poems—
A poem is it, neither he nor she. No, never
For you, yet, only for you; for him or for her,
Who is like unto these poems? No one other than
You—who else could it be? To be or not to be
A poem, a poet—who you are I will be I
Am everyone I have ever dreamed; *the stuff that
Dreams are made on.* Poets are dreamers, makers,
These dreams, all that seminal stuff we talk about—
I am no one I dream. This stuff —my dreams again—
Who comes, comes alone. These poems are especially
For you, of course they are for you. Who will accept
Them? Demand them? Command them? They are
                                        certainly
For you who will reject them—I do not want to be
Respected. These poems then are for everyone—
One who understands them—and he who never will.

WHITE NOISE

Jacob wrestles with his angel outside my window in the
lawn along the side of the path that snakes its way
between the buildings in the complex where I live,
another veil removed, worn again before me, how my
eyes, with them, I look at—I look to—the mirror with
dust, obliquely, another image of me, of you at your
vanity—I see you learning how to read the mirror; I have
read there myself and deeply, while I took photographs
with a stocking-sock pulled over the lens.

I have convinced myself that I must be as I must be,
standing as I stand before the mirror as I have stood—at
is not in, in is not on, new signs of how you struggle with
your likeness, the angel outside seems as if he is getting
the better of Jacob.

Who does not know he knows not himself, other signs
uncovered by my eyes, how I see your chest heave
slightly, looking as I do again obliquely, neither you nor I,
the mirror image, what we see between the stations, Alice
in the looking glass, no ripples, who is she?

I wonder aloud as a boy at a pond in the woods by Aunt
Anna Mae's, where I close my eyes and see you, hear you,
I do, an echo in my mind I imagine is my skull; eyes can
what they can, as if you were a poor mouse caught on a
glue trap.

Another woman, I see you speaking to me in the mirror,
all the grime that I see has collected from all the frying I
do in the summer.

TALKING DOES NOT COST MUCH

For Antonin Artaud and Il Poverello

I am talking to me as I do as
I have as I will continue perhaps,
How much does it cost me to talk as I do?
White sands, white sun, white noise — you are every
Woman, all others and no others. My
Wishing is not wanting, the mirror
With dust, what you said I could not wish for —
To wind up a man beside his own path.
I recall climbing the cliffs of Shadmoor
After searching the sands at Land's End,
Listening to Artaud on a rock
Reciting poetry he had written
Before the asylum, keeping accounts
With Francis — I try to count the drops that
Drip, blessed are the wounds for they shall bleed.
I reach a balance, the scars add up, no
Thing left for me to do as I have done
But to eat this miraculous ash.

QUESTIONS BEGET THEMSELVES

For Arthur Rimbaud

Between the sides light and dark, a candle's
Lit, the questions too flicker in the dark.
Candles set to see other than I turn
Again incandescently, I think again.
What is there to say, another rejoinder
At the ready, silence for silence offered,
Returned. What I have come to give, what more
Can be said in face of what I am able
To say. There is a *should* or *should not,* choice
Is prime — I have read the lyrics I should
Have read, themselves newly drawn questions
For the taking. There are always unusual
Limits put on responding for the present.

BEYOND PARTICIPATION

Other ladders have been raised to our
Window, outside on the lawn below
The window that looks east from my bedroom,
An angel appears just like that, just like
An angel would—just as angels have—
I am nothing like Jacob—I am not
This man Jacob. The lawn is brown, parched, burnt
Patches here and there, a checkerboard
By water scarce for weeks, I wish it would rain.
No rain today, to day or not to day,
The barometer tests new acrobatics.
Other ladders I place against other
Walls, brick walls outside, climbing up, climbing
Down—I watched Jacob and his angel, fixed
Eyes on the contest. I learn a lot
About the corner of my eye. Still as
A pillar, I love you—you stand. Post and
Lintel, elemental. Other words
Of wisdom I have at the ready,
A faith I bestow. We stow away,
Open window faithless, I see your
Silhouette on the wall, the shadows
Of your arms above your head, Epiphany
Has come, has gone, I see Sebastian full
Of holes, tied to the bedpost, imploring
As I do, although I have before.
I see that Sebastian sees me. He is
Between, as he becomes. I pause in the middle
Of things; I lay me down to sleep, to dream,
Maybe then to die, all sleep about death—
I used to pray as a boy, *Now I lay me*

Down to sleep . . . I look in my eyes in
The mirror and what I see that I see
Do you see . . . suddenly, still. It is
The Lord's to take, I might still believe.

I FALL TO PIECES

You do not reply when I ask, *What's*
In a name? I ask this question again.
I call out, *Martyrdom by any other* —
Martyrdom cannot be sweet. You remain
Mute, I turn to the bedpost, then back
To the mirror, the mirror opposite
The window, your eyes dead into mine. I
Say what I say, keeping silence a faith
I have lost. I see you shooting arrows
At Sebastian still tied to the bedpost.
Your silhouette rivals your shadow,
Another line drawing of Sebastian
By Lorca come to life. I watch as it
Walks about the room. Your silhouette strings
A bow: arrow after arrow comes at me.
The mirror image mine you miss. You hit
Sebastian, as I had suspected you
Would, the way you had with your eyes, shattered,
Suspicions, superstitions, definite
Lines drawn—lines are drawn. My drawers are full
Of freshly washed white socks, dried and folded
Neatly. I don't usually fall to pieces.

EGG ON THE FLOWERS

Eggshells make a garden grow I was told.
I recall how Humpty Dumpty, you know—
I do too. He does what he does, falls as
He falls, breaks as he breaks—I walk on eggshells
Around her. I hear horses at a gallop,
A rapid muffled pounding, their hooves coming
Like thunder, the breeze blows another
After alike, curtains going up,
Falling almost fully. Climbing again
Just as quickly when they fall nearly
Completely. All of a sudden, still. I
Drop out of bed; I shatter. I wish I
Never made fun of you doing jigsaw
Puzzles on the kitchen table. We used
To eat dinner in the living room. I
Ask you to piece me together. I was
Told that eggshells make a garden grow. I
Am put back together somehow, piece
By jagged piece—so do fish heads, I added,
I said to you, when you told me eggshells
Make a garden grow. I was told this
Once before, by an old Italian man,
All about how gardens grow, how eggshells
And fish heads and rotting banana
Peels, all of them are good for what you plant.

EQUILIBRIUM

I wish I knew how to wish I knew more
Than I know I know. Participation
Is voluntary even when coerced.
Does it matter if I agree? I carry
It without thinking, agreement is facile.
Day in, day out, clinging as I do
To vanity and hope; other clichés
I have come to live by; I pause to let
The funeral pass. What I wish for is
What I lack, my reputation for hope
Precedes me. The only time the body
Reaches equilibrium is when it
Is dead, dead friends dead relatives dead me.

A LESSON IN DYING

I watch a procession of the dead go by
On the shore at dawn,
One by one in single file,
Summer at Land's End,
Waves in offbeat rhythm silently rolling.
I draw dune flowers with a pencil,
Stick figure sketches of the ongoing parade,
Death carries the soul away, leads the way,
Why do I remember the story of Death?
All about Death — Death coming,
Death arriving — Death, the gentlest angel.
The dead carry lilies, I see the lilies I bought her —
Flowers of the Resurrection — Sickeningly sweet, she said.
Lilies are not for indoors, she said.
The plant I recall having bought one Easter,
Horribly cloying, she reminded me.
I see the lilies on the altar — falling petals,
Low Sunday. Everywhere around me,
The lilies and the dead . . .
Lilies having fallen faster than other years,
I think I recall the brown at the edges as they curled.
Gentle, the petals, the angel, yes, tender,
The Angel of Death is the gentlest angel,
I remember Fritz having said nothing about lilies.

SCAVENGERS

Another debate about sushi, what
To have for dinner. We decide
To eat mushroom pizza, as we also
Decide to watch night come at the shore — it
Rises, as I have said, does not descend —
In the east as the sun also rises
In the east. We finish our slices
Of pizza and stand on the shore at th'edge
Of low tide with the seagulls muffled
By the waves in succession one after
Another and another, night gray rising
From the east, turning black in time above
The horizon in the east, the gulls
Have gathered to scavenge the crabs left without
Cover. I pause to wonder the shells I've lived.

PEACEFUL MAY BE YOUR DEATH

I listen for words, carefully for words,
What they might tell me, what they could be,
What they are, how they become,
Always knowing I know more—
To forget is greedier than forgiving,
To give or to get, shades of gray shifting
Quickly at dusk. They talk to me,
Sleeping, I am sleeping—the dead talk to me.
To sleep or not to sleep
That might be what I think I could keep,
How I have made a place for them
To come and visit, and to talk again—
I do talk to the dead
In my dreams instead.

BY THEIR CANOPY

The woods are dark and remote, a forest
For the trees, deep shade by their canopy
In the day. The forest is thick with them,
The trees I walk past finding my way back
Home. Those who could have remembered have long
Forgotten. A dream I dreamed — it's always
About dreams — where one was one, and another,
Another. Everything depends on this
Addition, how one plus one equals two,
Plus one equals three. A popularly
Read edition — a late issue addition.

REST NO LONGER EYE

Truths remain tautological —
Having an I-to-I with me
With you. A chair is a chair is
A chair, just as a pig is a pig,
Not a woman, unless used as
A night table by the side
Of your bed — a stuffed pig, we
Remember, is a table. Do
You remember that function supplants
Form? Beauty can only exist
In form, a stuffed woman — form is
Truth is beauty, we know. Surely
Beauty in itself beauty can
Only take shape in form, I no
Longer rest; resting on my gaze —
Eye am I eyeing you, at what
Price, this dying peace, to be sold —
Should it be sold? Monologue after
Monologue going on and on
Inside, for the rest of me I hide.

BLT

Missing Mass for a Bacon Lettuce and
Tomato sandwich with mayo in the shop
On the corner of East Forty-fifth and D,
You're not supposed to chew the Communion
Wafer, I recall Monsignor Cross bellowing
From the steps leading to the altar
Of Saint Therese of Lisieux Church. I should
Have gone to mass—the bacon I loved. I
Did go to mass when I was a boy
Of seven, mother sending me cleaned and
Pressed, not yet pretending in the pews, all
Of us beneath the marble crucifix—
Was it stone? *Go in peace,* the priest said. I
See the cloves. I later imagined that
Therese's Jesus was plaster, a cast
Model on the cross, plaster cloves through plaster
Flesh with plaster blood in plaster spurts and
Plaster drops vividly from plaster wounds.

TEACHING ASSIGNMENT

Because I talk too much too often
To myself, the waiter brings me my soup
Quietly, I am frequently of one,
An audience, even amid others
Around me to see me I hear me when
I speak to others. I do wish I were
The Philosopher King. In their eyes—all reading
Intended to teach the reader how to die.
I recall I did not hear him approach,
The waiter in his stealth. I was not looking—
Looking away as I do, gazing ahead
At nowhere and nothing, eyes fixed. Seeing
Fastened, though, nonetheless—the eyes have it.
The soup he brought was white miso—I ask if
They ever have red. I recall the grace
Of red miso—an undergraduate—
How do we die? I wonder, I do. Does
Your reading teach you such things about death?

FRANK O'HARA

For Jacques Prevert

I finish my shrimp tempura
with spring roll,
salad and brown
rice.

I've already finished the miso soup
that comes with the lunch
at Yamato's.

The waitress comes to pour more green tea.

I ask for a small sake.

I wonder why she has to lift my cup
with her hand to pour
the tea.

I don't say anything to her.

I can't imagine she would understand.

I don't even imagine you do.

She then brings the sake
without pouring it.

MADE IN ORLEANS

Attention for the present comes sharply,
I am at ocean's edge, overcome
Overwhelmingly by the silver
Sinuosity of the wavelet tips,
Midmorning aluminum foil caps
In the sun, seagulls squawking as they do.
I have a dream, and in this dream I dream,
I am talking to Joan of Arc, only
Joan of Lorraine is Michelle Williams, her
Hair cut like Ingrid Bergman's. Why has no
One thought to cast Ms. Williams as the Maid
Of Orleans? I hand her the violets I have picked.
I stand watching her at the edge of the sea,
Waves, again, wings, once more; the petals
Of the violets in the wind. The day,
Beautiful in my dream, sun shining bright
As we have lunch near the harbor, sea scallops,
With Jimenez, with squid and a Galician
White. We discuss Joan of Lorraine, we do —
Jimenez reciting comparisons
Between sanctity and the sea — I heard
Garcia Lorca and Jimenez talk
Of a dream — I forget which one of them had dreamed
Of Joan of Lorraine, and how in this dream,
One of them kissed the Maid of Orleans
As I too kiss her in my dreams — touching
Bronze feet, the statue of her by the Seine —
We crush the violets between us.

HEADLONG

We had barbecue for dinner—chicken,
Steaks, burgers and dogs, I think my cousin
Had a beer—Buddy and his friend from Lowell,
Bobby Kennedy had yet to be shot.
Earlier that day, Riis Park before
Gateway National, long-line concessions,
How long did I wait for a hot dog
In the sun? *The Graduate* at the drive-in
In Pittsfield—how many hot dogs did I
Eat? I can see the heavy bulky metal
Speakers, dull gray, hanging on the window,
Stan's VW bus—I think it was red; his and
Clara's four kids and I in the back. We
Rode his convertible, Rockaway Beach,
Late Sixties, a British MG—
Cousin Buddy's summer travel. On the road,
Atlantic rising before us as we drive—
Top-down wind over the Marine Parkway
Bridge, Jamaica Bay. How old was I?
A boy burned to a crisp, my mother said.
It would be several years or more
Before I'd visit Lowell after his
Mother's funeral, my mother's mother's
Older sister Anna Mae. I walked the edge
Of the Merrimack that summer Aunt Anna
Died, in search of Kerouac's ghost, I think
I could have thought—I recall the sand
At low tide—I only recently found
Out Buddy died, seven years after the fact.
I see me diving headlong into a wave.

www.ingramcontent.com/pod-product-compliance
Lightning Source LLC
LaVergne TN
LVHW041306080426
835510LV00009B/881

9781939739889